PR
YOU
Pocketbook

C000212009

**By Brin Best,
Isabella Donnelly
& Macia Grebot**

Cartoons:
Phil Hailstone

Published by:

Teachers' Pocketbooks
Laurel House, Station Approach,
Alresford, Hampshire SO24 9JH, UK
Tel: +44 (0)1962 735573
Fax: +44 (0)1962 733637
E-mail: sales@teacherspocketbooks.co.uk
Website: www.teacherspocketbooks.co.uk

*Teachers' Pocketbooks is an imprint of
Management Pocketbooks Ltd.*

All rights reserved. No part of this publication
may be reproduced, stored in a retrieval
system or transmitted in any form, or by any
means, electronic, mechanical, photocopying,
recording or otherwise, without the prior
permission of the publishers.

© Brin Best, Isabella Donnelly &
Macia Grebot 2006.

This edition published 2006.

ISBN 9 781903 776667
ISBN 1 903776 66 X

British Library Cataloguing-in-Publication
Data – A catalogue record for this book is
available from the British Library.

Design, typesetting and graphics by Efex Ltd.
Printed in UK.

Contents

Devising and Implementing Your Strategy — Getting your strategy right, recognising existing work, high status and congruence, headteacher's role, students' role, stakeholder liaison, the 12-step framework from agreeing and implementing your vision to evaluating, modifying and revisiting — **11**

Managing the Media — The power of the media, understanding how it works, contacts, getting organised, news releases, monitoring, evaluating and improving coverage, radio and television, dealing with the media in a crisis — **49**

Promotional Opportunities — The role of promotional material, the prospectus, the school newsletter, using and developing the website, open events, work in the community, managing the parental grapevine, easily missed opportunities — **79**

School Case Studies — Real examples showing how eight different schools successfully promoted themselves or improved their image — **97**

Self-evaluation Tool — Use the self-evaluation tool to assess the current situation, identify what you need to do and judge progress — **107**

Introduction

Some schools always seem to be in the news with good stories about their achievements. People speak **positively** about these schools, parents want to send their children there, and there is a feel-good factor about them. Such schools are confident and outgoing in their approach; they ooze success.

Other schools find it hard to get good media coverage, or even worse, often seem to get **negative** stories printed about them. People are wary of these schools, reluctant to send their children there and feel – rightly or wrongly – that such places are simply not up to scratch. These schools find it difficult to be positive in their outlook and often look for short-term, quick fixes for their problems, which do not help.

The schools that fall into the first category aren't necessarily the best funded or highest performing in the leafy suburbs. They're the ones that have learnt how to **manage** their public profile.

Introduction

This book explains how to ensure your school makes the most of its achievements. It describes an accessible, practical **strategy** to help you transform the way your school is perceived. Clear instructions, and a range of tools and techniques, guide you through the steps to take so that your school can enjoy the kind of positive profile enjoyed by the select few.

As well as practical guidance on how to raise the profile of your school, we've included **case studies** of a range of schools that have succeeded in making a real difference to the way they're perceived. Many have emerged from challenging circumstances to enjoy acclaim in their communities.

The book concludes with a **self-evaluation tool** to help you highlight what needs to be done next in your bid to gain the positive profile your school deserves.

Introduction

Creating a positive identity and promoting your school effectively is all about improving the school's reputation, raising its profile and contributing to its success. There are many reasons for promoting your school, even if you think its image is currently quite good in your community:

- Schools with a positive image tend to have better student behaviour and higher attendance rates
- Creating a buzz about your school can energise staff and students, improve morale and promote pride in the school
- Creating a positive identity fosters a sense of belonging
- A school that has a positive image will find it easier to retain staff
- Promotional work can provide a focus for the celebration of all the successful things you do

It's worth bearing in mind that some schools that have emerged from serious challenges have found the effective promotion of their image a key **driving force** for school improvement. The power of a positive image should not be underestimated.

Introduction

We have written the book with a variety of readers in mind:

- Headteachers (the role of the head as the school's top ambassador is vital), senior leaders, and governors who are responsible for whole school issues
- Other school staff who have been given responsibility for coordinating work on promoting the school
- Staff wishing to know how they can play their part in raising the profile of the school (eg subject leaders, teachers, support staff)

Introduction

This book:

- Gives you a thorough grounding in the principles of effective marketing and public relations work
- Helps you devise an appropriate strategy to raise your school's profile
- Gives a wealth of practical advice on the day-to-day issues underpinning your work
- Provides a structured path to improving your school's profile through a self-evaluation tool
- Outlines the roles of key people in improving your school's image

Introduction

Everyone from the headteacher to the students has a part to play in helping to promote your school. Students can be powerful ambassadors and through their achievements can help to raise a school's profile.

Although the book suggests a step-by-step approach to devising a marketing and public relations* strategy, it cannot go further and actually create the vision that will drive this. This is where you'll need to take over – but we'll guide you along the way with down-to-earth advice and a range of tools to make the job easier.

Remember
You need to agree a vision and strategy that is appropriate to your **particular** school, bearing in mind your own priorities and local circumstances. There's no 'one size fits all' strategy that you can take off the shelf and use tomorrow. Instead, we provide you with an overall framework to help you build your own strategy.

*Marketing – attracting students and parents to your school and retaining their loyalty and support.
PR – the professional maintenance of a favourable public image.

Introduction

To get the most out of this book, be **bold** with your vision, and implement the actions designed to get you there with **enthusiasm**, **determination** and **energy**. These four factors will make a huge difference.

In taking forward the ideas here it will also make a big difference if you can assemble a marketing/PR group. Later in the book we suggest that one person should head up this group as overall coordinator. Having a supportive team working alongside the coordinator will be vital to success.

We have been encouraged and energised by the schools we have worked with and are convinced that amazing things are possible with appropriate vision and commitment from all members of the school community.

Devising and Implementing Your Strategy

Managing the Media

Promotional Opportunities

School Case Studies

Self-evaluation Tool

Devising and Implementing Your Strategy

Getting your strategy right

The numbers on the clock face opposite represent the 12 steps of our framework (explored in detail on pages 19 – 48) for building and revising a marketing/PR strategy for your school. It may also be seen as a marketing/PR cycle.

The work must be given **high status**, with the full support and participation of the headteacher, senior management and governors.

Effective **communication** and liaison with internal and external stakeholders is vital at every stage of the process, and **training** – which could range from one-to-one work to group sessions – will be required at different stages.

Getting your strategy right

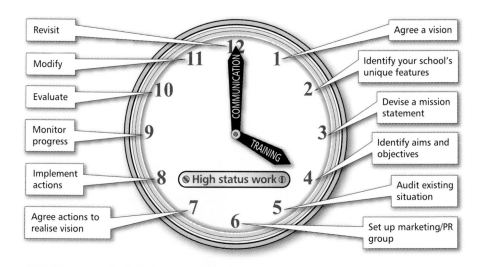

- Revisit
- Modify
- Evaluate
- Monitor progress
- Implement actions
- Agree actions to realise vision

COMMUNICATION

TRAINING

High status work

- Agree a vision
- Identify your school's unique features
- Devise a mission statement
- Identify aims and objectives
- Audit existing situation
- Set up marketing/PR group

Recognising existing work

You'll find that there is **already** a range of valuable marketing activities being carried out by your school (eg the school prospectus, parents' evenings, school fair, open days, newsletters) and by various individuals. You may have already carried out audits and surveys and know exactly what your profile is in the local community.

This chapter will help you determine where you are in a marketing/PR cycle and how to ensure that your school continues in its long-term commitment to this work. The strategy you devise will ensure that activities are planned throughout the academic year and that there is ongoing research, feedback, quality control and evaluation.

High status and congruence

In developing and implementing a marketing/PR plan, you are embracing school development at every level by recognising parents and students as users who have a choice. This guarantees the work is given high status.

However, any drive to improve the public profile of your school requires that senior staff and governors consider it a **high priority**. It's essential to have their full and active support if you are to be effective. This could include:

- Publicly declaring their support when the project is launched
- Making time to discuss the issues at staff/governor meetings
- Being powerful advocates for the work in their dealings with staff and others
- Providing quotes for news releases
- Being prepared to meet people to promote the school

Once your PR work is underway keep a close eye on **congruence**. Ensure that all marketing and communications developments are consistent with the vision, mission statement and ethos of the school; that they reflect stakeholders' needs; that they present a clear view of what the school is trying to do. They should enable any 'ambassador' to explain the common purpose of the school.

The key role of the headteacher

Many parents will judge a school, and indeed decide whether or not the school is right for their child, based on their impression of the headteacher. In short, the headteacher is the face of a school and has an intrinsic role in promoting it. Make the most of the headteacher as the key public relations figure by:

- Ensuring he/she is visibly involved in daily routines, eg bus duty, greeting students at the start of the day, being present at sports matches, concerts and plays
- Ensuring his/her presence at open events – prospective parents will want to see the head, hear him/her speak and have the opportunity for a personal discussion
- Welcome messages in your website, prospectus and newsletters – this will help parents get a feel for the head's personality and reinforce the 'capable strong leader' message
- Setting up a weekly 'headteacher's clinic/question time' for parents and/or students
- Considering how to develop relationships with feeder schools

The students' role

Your students are also vital assets in promoting the image of your school.
Everything they do, both in school and in the wider community, can have an effect on
how your school is perceived. Make sure they're aware of their role in
marketing their school and maintaining a positive public profile.

- Involve them in vision-building exercises to ensure that their views have been taken into account
- Make the most of their positive achievements in your own publications and through the media
- Include examples of their work in publicity materials
- Ensure that when out and about in the local community, especially while wearing school uniform, students are mindful of what impression they give of the school

Stakeholder liaison

It's critical to involve all stakeholders in devising and implementing your strategy. If people are consulted and told that their views are important, then they will be far more likely to embrace and accept changes, play their part in bringing them about and encourage others to do the same.

Such consultation is also important because schools can only be effective if they reflect the needs of both their immediate and wider communities. This can be achieved by:

- Including people when building the vision
- Opening up meetings
- Holding briefings
- Issuing written updates
- Sharing all plans
- Ensuring **all** views are listened to and respected

Effective **communication** is the key to stakeholder liaison.

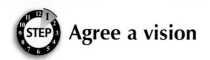 **Agree a vision**

The importance of vision

Schools are terrifically busy and high-pressure places in which to work, and it often seems that there's little time to stop, think and consider where you are heading.

When beginning any new initiative you need to put time aside to consider the **big picture** and agree a vision for the kind of school you want to become. This is an empowering and exciting exercise, as it allows you to focus on a future which is 'ideal'. It will help you to describe where you want to be as a school – a place which is more successful and more fulfilling for everyone.

Agreeing a vision will also make clear your specific goals – your aims and objectives – and help to reveal the steps you need to take to make them a reality – your actions.

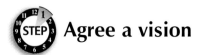 **Agree a vision**

Building the vision

To build your vision, take the following steps:

1. Working in small groups, imagine it is five years in the future – this is a reasonable timescale in which to work.
2. Imagine how you would like your school to be perceived five years hence, eg how will people talk about your school, or how will it be reported in the press?
3. Write down statements which describe this future specifically
4. Discuss these statements among the groups and then with the wider audience.

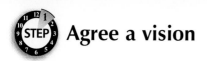 **Agree a vision**

Building the vision

5. Summarise the statements of all participants in the exercise in a suitable format.
   It could be a diagram, mind map or clusters of ideas. The aim is to get the
   'essence' of the ideas by synthesising the main points.

6. Prepare a written description of your vision that makes it clear where you want to
   be in five years – use active and positive language to make this upbeat and
   exciting, eg *'Our school is...', 'Our students are...', 'Our parents believe...',
   'Our community thinks...'* etc.

A collaborative approach called logovisual thinking is especially suited to this kind of
vision building (see www.changeandinnovation.com for details).

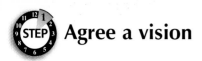 **Agree a vision**

An inclusive vision

The most robust visions are those that benefit from the input of all the key **stakeholders**. Although the headteacher and senior management team are ultimately responsible for determining and driving forward the vision in collaboration with governors, consider who else should be involved:

- Teaching staff
- Non-teaching staff
- Parents
- Students
- Governors
- Community representatives

There are various ways to bring together these people to formulate the vision, but the most effective methods will generally involve informal meetings where much small group **discussion** is encouraged.

Identify unique features

Your vision will identify things that need to **change** for you to become a more effective school. But don't lose sight of the fact that you **already** do some things very well and will need to make the most of these positive features:

- In all your work, stress the unique features of your school
- Find ways to weave these positive messages into all marketing materials
- Make sure your vision doesn't seek to change everything – some areas of the school will already be highly effective

The unique features of your school will help you to devise an upbeat motto or strapline, which can form the basis of a highly effective campaign – this is dealt with in step 3.

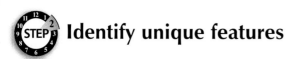 # Identify unique features

The following SWOT (strengths, weaknesses, opportunities, threats) analysis will help you to think in more detail about your school's **strengths** and **weaknesses**.

Ask the school's stakeholders (see page 22), ideally working in mixed groups, to identify strengths, weaknesses, opportunities and threats. Ask individuals to turn identified weaknesses into possible opportunities for the school, both internally and externally.

This exercise will help you to identify the **unique selling points** or features of your school and the key messages you want to communicate to the internal and external school community. Make sure they are written down so that everyone is clear about what they are. An example of a SWOT analysis is included on the following page.

Identify unique features

Strengths

Excellent facilities, eg sports, school library.
Positive working environment.
Respect between students and staff.
Caring, dedicated and committed teachers.
Strong leadership.

Weaknesses

Negative stories in local press.
PTA not very active or non-existent.
Sports facilities not used to full potential.
Below national average test results.
Lack of extra-curricular activities.

Opportunities

Press campaign, promoting good news stories
about the school in the local press.
Getting parents into school via various events
and involving them more in school activities.
Monthly newsletter for parents.
Introduce more sports clubs.
Get PTA involved in new activities.

Threats

A new school opening down the road in the
next academic year.
Falling results.
Falling roll.
Poor behaviour on local streets and buses at
home time.

STEP 3 Devise a mission statement

Your school's mission statement should articulate your vision and communicate the unique features of your school. It will be one of the hardest things to capture in a simple sentence or paragraph – but it's vital to produce one. Be clear and concise, encapsulating the essence of the school, its aims and its values, eg:

Check new developments against your mission statement to ensure that:

- They are consistent with the vision
- They give a clear view of what the school is trying to do
- They enable any 'ambassador' to clearly explain the school's common purpose
- There is a clear understanding of the stakeholder needs

STEP 3 Identify aims and objectives

Identifying the **aims** and **objectives** of your strategy will provide some direction by helping you to clarify what you're trying to achieve and what's appropriate for a marketing/PR group to take on. During this stage:

- Set specific **aims** to help achieve your vision, aims which fall within the remit of the marketing/PR group

- Consider how your aims relate to the school development/improvement plan and commit to building them into that plan if they aren't already there

- Agree **protocols** for the work (eg who you are prepared to work with, how you will operate, the ethics underpinning your work, etc)

Remember that your marketing/PR work is just one aspect of the process by which you will create positive change in your school. The marketing/PR group's role is to drive and manage the communication process that supports and enables the work of the school as it moves towards achieving its vision. To realise the vision other people will need to act too (eg the leadership group, subject teams, teachers).

Identify aims and objectives

Aims

From the vision and the mission statement, your school can develop a range of aims that should meet its general and specific requirements. The next step is to focus on each aim and decide on more specific objectives and actions that will ensure the vision is realised.

Examples of general aims

'We will create a better image of the school and improve its profile in the community.'
'We will inform parents and strive to involve them in the life of the school.'
'We will tackle any negative perceptions of the school.'

Examples of specific aims

'We will increase intake by 5% compared with the current year by 2008.'
'90% of parents will see us as the automatic choice for their children in this community.'
'We will be recognised as a leader in the area of ICT in learning by at least 75% of parents.'

STEP Identify aims and objectives

Objectives

After identifying the school's aims, the objectives can then be more focused, making clear how the aims are to be achieved. As in any effective plan, the objectives should be SMART – specific, measurable, achievable, relevant and timed.

Below are two examples of objectives associated with the general aims on the previous page:

1. Find out about all the local media in the community.
2. Increase the number of press releases issued by the school.

Pages 39-41 show how these can be turned into actions.

 **Audit**

Once you have an exciting vision of the future and a clear idea of the aims and objectives which underpin it, it's tempting to begin work straight away to try to make that future a reality. But first you need to take stock of how the school is **currently perceived** in your community.

This is an important opportunity to gather high quality evidence that will help you plan your strategy. It will show the extent of the work required, and where your efforts most need to be targeted.

But be warned – if you've not done this exercise before you may be surprised by the results! To make meaningful change you'll need to be open to the views and opinions of others (even if you don't agree with them!). You'll soon realise that your own impression of how your school is perceived is only part of the picture – indeed, other people may not share it.

 **Audit**

Research will help your school evaluate its strengths and weaknesses and assess the effectiveness of its existing communications, thereby contributing to an **audit** of your current profile.

As part of this audit it's vital to review all your publications, consider who receives them and decide whether the range should be broadened (see next page).

Key information that the school should analyse to help identify actions includes:

- Results of questionnaires and attitude surveys from all key stakeholders
- Feedback from focus groups
- Feedback from parents, staff, and a SWOT analysis (see page 24 Step 2)
- Ofsted reports
- PANDAs and other performance and assessment data
- School self-evaluation programmes
- Analysis of events such as open evenings by people whose judgement you value

 **Audit**

Use a table like the example filled in below to analyse your **target audience** and how you currently communicate with them.

Target audience	Communications
Current parent body	Regular (weekly/monthly) school newsletter, website, local press
Feeder school parents	Prospectus, open evening, open morning, induction events, website, local press, holiday programmes
Feeder school staff	School newsletter, visits, mentoring programme
Students in link/feeder schools	Regular visits to your school, induction events
Community as a whole	Combination of above

 **Audit**

There are various other **sources** of evidence to which you should refer when building a picture of your current profile:

- Staff views (teaching and non-teaching)
- Parents' views
- Governors' views
- Students' views
- How you are portrayed in the media

Do not neglect the **general community** surrounding your school. Such people as local shopkeepers, bus drivers and residents living near the school often have important and sometimes influential views of your school.

 **Audit**

You can use a wide range of methods to gather the **evidence** you need to judge how your school is currently perceived:

The exact mixture of techniques you use will depend on the amount of time you have to devote to this activity and the particular circumstances of your school. **But remember**, the wider the variety of data collection techniques you use, the more comprehensive a picture you will be able to build.

 # **Audit**

Simple **questionnaires** can be an excellent way to gather high quality information about your school quickly. Consider the following questions:

- What are the school's strengths?
- What are the school weaknesses? These will present opportunities
- How is the school perceived in the general community?
- What kind of press coverage does the school get in the local newspapers?
- How well does the school communicate with students, parents and the wider community?
- Are there any threats facing your school? eg new school build in the area, change in staffing levels, changing demographics

Though setting up and analysing the results of this sort of exercise will obviously take time, it will give you invaluable data on which to form more accurate judgements about your school.

 **Audit**

You can investigate your media profile in an **analytical** way by using the template opposite. It allows you to gather information on how your school is portrayed. By giving a score to each article, you can assess how positive or negative reporting on your school has been over a set period of time, and judge progress in the future. You will need to gather cuttings – both good and bad – on your school over some months in order to carry out this exercise properly.

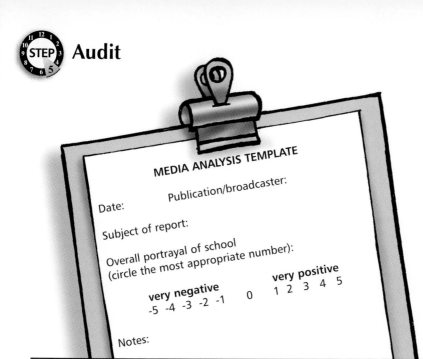

STEP 5 Audit

MEDIA ANALYSIS TEMPLATE

Date: Publication/broadcaster:

Subject of report:

Overall portrayal of school
(circle the most appropriate number):

very negative   **very positive**
-5 -4 -3 -2 -1   0   1 2 3 4 5

Notes:

Set up a marketing/PR group

A **group** should now be established that has responsibility for your school's marketing/PR work and a coordinator appointed to take the lead. Have on the team:

- At least one member of the senior management team
- A governor
- A member of non-teaching staff
- A parent
- A community representative

The role of the group is to develop, plan, monitor and evaluate the progress of the marketing/PR work. By identifying members' roles and responsibilities you can ensure you are making the most of the team's skills and experience. The group should meet on at least a half-termly basis for a focused meeting with an agenda. Some schools pay a marketing/PR coordinator to maximise work in this area.

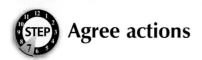 # STEP 5 Agree actions

By this step the marketing/PR group will have the outcome of research and input from all stakeholders; they will now be ready to agree an **action plan**. This should refer directly to the objectives identified in step 4. To produce a robust action plan, create a list of priorities of both internal and external requirements. Make reference to the school calendar, along with key admission dates to help identify these actions.

The plan should make clear the **timetable** for the work, the actions required and any associated costs, who is responsible for doing what and how the work will be **monitored** (progress checked) and **evaluated** (outcomes assessed). **Success criteria** will help you to judge whether the actions have been carried out effectively. This can be laid out in tabular form as in the examples on the next pages.

The group will also need to find or establish a quick and effective internal system to share success and good news stories. This will facilitate external communication. Once you've put the plan together, share it with the people who need to see it: all staff and governors.

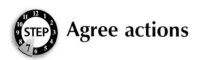 # Agree actions

The following tables show two example objectives listed with a range of linked
actions, thereby constituting a mini development plan for each objective:

Find out about the local media in the community

Action	Responsibility	Cost	Timing	Monitoring	Evaluation	Success criteria
Research local newspapers, magazines, radio and TV stations						
Search the internet for key community websites						
Research editorial deadline dates, etc						
Prepare a schedule with all this information						

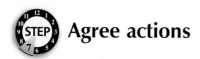 **Agree actions**

Increase the number of press releases issued by the school

Action	Responsibility	Cost	Timing	Monitoring	Evaluation	Success criteria
Check the school diary for key events to be promoted						
Produce a draft schedule with a half-termly programme of press releases						
Assign responsibility for writing and sending out releases						
Ensure digital photos are taken to accompany releases						

 # Implement actions

It helps to prepare a **yearly** schedule with **termly** actions. Members of the group will have their individual actions or will possibly meet with a sub-group to ensure activities/events are organised according to the plan and that deadlines are met. Here's a simplified schedule – remember that some things (eg issuing press releases) should take place on a regular basis throughout the year.

	Autumn term	Spring term	Summer term
Print and publications	School prospectus Promotional leaflet/poster	Newspaper supplement	School logo Headed paper, etc
Advertising	Open event	Recruitment of staff	Summer fair
Public relations	Regular news stories	Advertorial	Photocalls
Special events	Open days/evenings	Specialist status - launch	Local competitions
Website	Development of contents	Website update	Review contents
Research	Student questionnaire	Staff survey	Parental focus groups
Primary links	Roadshows in schools	Half-termly newsletter	Workshops for year 4/5
Internal communications	Staff briefing	School newsletter	Update display boards
Business links	Developing local business links and researching sponsorship opportunities		

 **Monitor progress**

Monitoring your marketing/PR strategy and activities throughout the year is an important element of the process. It involves checking that things are **progressing** according to plan.

Think about the monitoring systems you currently have in place and whether they can be improved or increased. For example:

- Is the school receptionist asking where parental telephone enquirers heard about the school?
- Does the school website have a feedback section?
- Could questionnaires asking for parental/community feedback from all school events/activities be introduced?

All information collected should be passed to the marketing/PR coordinator.

 # Evaluate

Evaluation is concerned with the degree to which you've been **successful**. It should take place at least once a term, measuring the results and learning from them. Look at any statistics or evidence that will help the evaluation process:

- Has staff attendance improved?
- What's staff turnover like?
- What are the application figures for staff recruitment?
- How many visitors has your website received?
- How many organisations do you have links with?
- How many events are there and how many people turn up to them?
- What is the range of telephone enquiries you've received?

 **Evaluate**

Measures that could demonstrate success (and things to aim for next) include:

- The student roll has stabilised (start looking at how to increase numbers of applicants)
- Press coverage is increasing (is there any way this could lead to higher-profile coverage?)
- Staff retention rates are improving (what about the quality of staff at recruitment?)
- There are improved links with external organisations (is this leading to more sponsorship or high quality work experience opportunities?)
- There are increased numbers at events (is this translating into higher numbers of first choice applications or more positive perceptions in the community?)

Regular monitoring and evaluation will ensure that successful projects lead to higher aims.

 **Evaluate**

Marketing/PR activities can be broken down for evaluation purposes:

Area for evaluation	Examples of specific things to review
Publications	New colour school prospectus, direct mailshots
Media	Closer liaison with local press
Events	Environment day in the community, events linked to local shops and business associations, involvement in community events
Research	Annual survey to local community, staff survey/focus groups
Photography	Review whether the school has a stock of good quality photographs (digital)
Primary links	Existing links/projects with feeder schools
Internal communications	Parents/wider community, staff
External communications	Stories in press and community newsletters

 **Modify**

In the light of your evaluation, how could your marketing/PR work be modified to increase its effectiveness? The marketing group should consider the following questions about the activities that were planned for the previous year:

- Which were completed?
- How was progress monitored?
- What factors contributed to their completion according to the plan?
- Which were not completed?
- Why were they not completed?
- How can the situation be rectified?
- How effective are the outcomes in achieving the aims?
- What was really successful and can be repeated next year?
- What was really successful and can be expanded on next year?
- What promotional activity will you never do again? Why?

The answers will help inform the strategy for the following year.

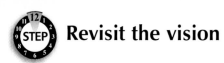 # Revisit the vision

Every few years **revisit** the vision and carry out the exercise outlined in step 1 again. Priorities change, initiatives come and go, institutions evolve – so there's a need to step back from the cut and thrust of your marketing/PR work to connect again with the big picture.

Once again, a range of key stakeholders needs to be involved in the exercise. It should be a welcome and inspirational task, as much new work will have been carried out in the intervening time to make the school a better place. Now you are focusing on how to aim even higher!

Devising and Implementing Your Strategy

 Managing the Media ◀

 Promotional Opportunities

 School Case Studies

 Self-evaluation Tool

Managing the Media

The power of the media

The media can have a very powerful effect on how your school is perceived, so it's vital that effective **media relations** form an integral part of your marketing/PR strategy. The media are especially important to schools because:

- They are one of the main outlets for getting information about your school into the public domain
- They help people form opinions about your school
- If you develop positive working relationships with the media they can be strong advocates for your work
- They are one of the cheapest and most effective ways of getting your message across to your stakeholders and the general community
- If students and staff see themselves in the press on a regular basis it will improve morale and self-esteem

However, there are also pitfalls for the unwary and a carefully coordinated and managed approach is called for.

Understanding how it works

The media industry in the UK does not enjoy a great deal of popularity among many teachers. Inaccurate reporting, complaints about teachers' long holidays and negative stories about the strife of modern schools all contribute to its unpopularity.

Yet, for the most part, the press – especially newspapers – actually contain many more **positive** stories about schools than negative ones. It's just that the bad news stories tend to stick in the mind longer than the good ones!

Newspaper editors and other decision-makers in the media industry don't wish to fill their pages with bad news and don't have a vendetta against schools. It's simply that many news stories they latch on to have a negative bias, so it's up to you to send good news their way. This clearly presents an **opportunity** for your school and is a reminder of how your students and their achievements are key assets when it comes to PR.

Understanding how it works

If you make it easy for journalists to report good news about your school, then the positive stories will follow.

You can make their job easier by:

- Having one named media/press contact at your school and at the media outlet
- Sending a regular flow of high quality news releases
- Inviting the press to photo calls and other events
- Sending in the latest stories or breaking news according to the preferred method of the media outlet (eg fax, phone, email)

Remember also to keep tabs on the **copy deadlines** for local weekly papers, which can be an ideal outlet for your stories. If you set up effective systems, you will soon have journalists ringing you up for stories!

Making and sustaining contacts

It's very useful to have **named contacts** within the media industry, people you've met and with whom you've built up positive relationships. And, as news these days comes in many forms – television, radio, the printed press and the internet – aim to exploit all avenues.

- It's perfectly acceptable to phone your local newspapers and invite journalists, or even the editor, to your school to give out prizes at prize giving, work with students on projects or simply for a chat

- Newspapers have many pages to fill every week, and most journalists are happy to increase their own contacts with news sources

- Ensure journalists and photographers are regularly invited into school to cover events, eg fundraising, special visitors, school productions

- Try to set up interesting and unusual photos rather than standard 'cheque presentation' type shots

Making and sustaining contacts

You can organise your media contacts list by using a **template** such as the one below. Include local media outlets, plus national education magazines, newspapers, TV and radio so that when a really big story breaks you are ready.

Publication/radio station, etc.	Copy deadline	Contact person	Phone/ fax number	Email address	Postal address

Getting organised

Be **proactive**. By paying close attention to the school calendar one term in advance you can spot media opportunities and **plan ahead**. Pre-planning stories in this way allows you to help steer the news agenda in the direction you want it to go, rather than being reactive and sending in whatever stories you have in a particular week.

If you're organised it's possible to get more than one story from an event, eg

Drama production:

- Public appeal for unusual prop
- Response to above
- Review of the play

Community/inter-school event:

- Planning and pre-publicity
- Press coverage on the day
- Community reactions

News releases

News releases are a key way to get information into the open about your school.

- Send them to newspapers, radio and television
- Use them as updates on your school website
- Use them to help compile regular newsletters and/or end of year annual review
- Display them where they can be seen by the school community and by visitors (but make sure they are kept up to date)
- Keep them in a file as a record of key events at your school

Writing news releases is something of a **skill** in itself, but there are simple rules to follow and you soon get better at writing them. Sooner or later you will get the thrill of seeing an article in a newspaper based on your news release, and from time to time it will not even be altered from your original text!

As it makes the job of editing so much easier, many newspapers now welcome news releases via email. *Find out how your local newspapers prefer to receive theirs.*

Writing a news release

General guidance:

- A news release must contain news!
- Consider why and for whom the information is interesting
- The news release draws attention to the bigger story and should highlight the most interesting elements:

  What

  Where

  When

  Why

  Who

- Keep your sentences and paragraphs short, factual and jargon-free, explaining any acronyms (HOD, AST etc) you use

Writing a news release

- Try to use the name of the school in the opening sentence for maximum impact, eg Grange Primary School is celebrating...

- Give the story to someone else to proofread for spelling and grammatical accuracy as well as content

- There are times when a story isn't strong enough to stand on its own but a good picture will carry it. Generally, stories are likely to get better coverage if accompanied by a photograph, so have completed photography permission forms for all your students in advance and remember that the quality of the photo can make a big difference. (Avoid low quality digital images)

- Follow up your news release with a telephone call to the local newspaper to chek that they have received it and to ask when they will publish it.

Using photos

An image can sell a story, so:

- Check how media outlets prefer these –
  printed photos, slides, digital images
- Be clear about whether reproduction will
  be in black and white or colour, as this
  affects picture composition and lighting
- Stage the photo but avoid rows of
  students and crowd shots – maximum
  three people in each image
- Look at the background and be aware of
  what is happening behind the image (fire
  exits blocked, inappropriate displays,
  health and safety issues, etc)
- Think about close-ups – facial expressions
  can provide very powerful images
- Ensure pictures are accurately captioned,
  eg *'Pictured left to right are ...'*

Sample news release

NEWS RELEASE

30 September 2006
For immediate use

HILLTOP HIGH STUDENTS WIN TOP SCIENCE AWARD

Hilltop High School is celebrating another major achievement after two Year 10 students were declared Regional Young Scientists of the Year in a prestigious competition sponsored by the National Science Foundation.

Samie Jones and Lee-Roy Blackwell, both 14, have been honoured for their investigation into the effect of caffeine on the human body. They will both receive a £25 book voucher as a prize, together with a special certificate to mark their success.

Head of science, Sunita Clarke, said: 'We are delighted that the hard work of our students has been recognised in this way. Samie and Lee-Roy's entry was outstanding and we are confident they have the potential for a career in science'.

Always write 'news release' at the top

Include date for release of story

Keep headline short and simple – leave clever puns to the editor!

Most important points, including school's name, at start of story

First paragraph should summarise story in a sentence. (Study newspaper intros to get the idea.)

Include a quote to enhance story (Draft one for approval by the source if they're unsure what to say.)

Sample news release

Head of science, Sunita Clarke, said: "We are delighted that the hard work of our students has been recognised in this way. Sanna and Lee-Roy's entry was outstanding and we are confident they have the potential for a career in science'.

ENDS

Photo opportunity
12:30 pm on 6 October in the main foyer at the school on Westhead Lane, with the students, their certificates and the head of science. Please telephone to confirm attendance.

Further information
For additional information, or to arrange an interview with Mrs Clarke, please phone Alistair Campbell (school press officer) on 0118 4535590 during office hours and 0777 1122352 outside those hours.
Email: bigal@hilltop.sch.uk.

Put ENDS at foot of news release

Consider offering a photo opportunity

Include contact details for further information

Format
- On school headed notepaper
- Double line spacing
- Margins should be at least 2.5 cm allowing for ease of reading and editors to make notes
- Content on one side of the page only
- Whenever possible, attach captioned photograph(s) (preferably digital if using email)

Monitoring and evaluating coverage

It is important to **monitor** press and media coverage about your school to determine whether your news releases result in stories and to see how those stories are reported.

- Keep a record of all news releases issued
- Make sure you get copies of all local newspapers on a weekly basis (either subscribe or ask staff/parents to bring a copy to school)
- Cut out the press coverage and add publication date and name of newspaper
- Keep a record of all coverage the school receives in a cuttings book, with a copy in your school reception
- Create a 'good news board' on which all positive press coverage is displayed, making sure it's located where staff, students and the community will see it

The media analysis template on page 37 provides a systematic way of evaluating coverage and can be used to track it over a set period of time.

Improving coverage

If the school is not receiving the media coverage it deserves, then you need to act. Try the following:

- Double-check the contact details of all journalists and newspapers
- Ensure you are sending the release and/or photograph in the format they require
- Telephone the journalists a couple of days prior to the event or to the release being issued
- Follow up to ensure they received your release
- Speak to the editor – local newspapers are there to support and inform the community and your school is an important source of information. This can also stimulate interest in your school: don't waste any opportunity to talk about the latest interesting project
- If you have a school newsletter make sure media outlets receive a copy – it keeps your school in the spotlight
- Ask for permission to use newspaper photos in your newsletter/prospectus as it helps to develop the link in the public mind

Radio and television

Local **radio** and **television** are well worth considering as a means of reaching a wide audience. Both are potentially interested in news stories from schools, though getting involved with broadcast media can often be rather time-consuming.

Radio stations are ideal if you want to make appeals, or are able to go on air to talk about a story. It's advantageous if your school has somebody who's relatively at ease speaking with the media. Radio interviews can often be done over the phone, and as many are not recorded live they're frequently edited in a flattering way for the speaker. (Umms, ahhs, and mistakes edited out). But find out before if it will be live.

If you're ready to take on the challenge of getting your school on TV, then there are rich rewards. However, it can take a whole afternoon to get a few seconds of film, and it's often necessary to stage-manage situations for the camera, which is not everyone's cup of tea. It also needs plenty of advance notice on both sides.

Dealing with the media in a crisis

Although you'll hopefully never have to deal with one, it's worth starting at the beginning and considering, what exactly is a crisis?

They come in different forms, are usually sudden, and tend to fall into one of the following categories:

- The unexpected, unpredictable, out of the blue

- The issue that is known but is not yet public

- The issue that everyone else seems to know about before you do

Crisis? What crisis?

Examples could include:

- Death or serious injury to a student or member of staff
- A serious allegation against a member of staff that has become public
- Fire, natural hazard or building failure posing a serious risk
- A student involved in an accident on a school trip
- School party becoming caught up in a major incident (national or international) eg ferry disaster, bomb explosion, hijack/siege

Whichever, you can be pretty sure that the available information may be uncertain or unreliable and the situation may develop in a way that gives you little time to respond.

If students are involved, be particularly aware of the impact on families. Make sure that what they hear from school is consistent so the media can't exploit variations in information.

When things go wrong

So what do you do?

- Say nothing?
- Batten down the hatches?
- Blame it on someone else?
- Close the school?
- Run for cover?
- Or take control and manage it?

Because you can be sure that if a crisis occurs, it will do so at the worst possible time and your priority will be to deal with the problem itself.

Be prepared

The key to effective crisis management is to be prepared! You will not have much time to react and once the incident has taken place it's too late to think, let alone plan. So get planning now. Ensure your school has procedures in place for managing this kind of incident. Know what has to be done and who is going to do it.

A crisis always demands a quick response and badly handled it can threaten your school's reputation. A well-managed response, however, can not only preserve that reputation, it can enhance it.

Have a **crisis plan** for handling the media in the event of a major incident affecting your school – make sure *all* staff and governors are aware of it (there's nothing worse than an ill-informed loose canon). The headteacher should be the person to take the lead in such incidents.

The media crisis plan

Your media crisis plan can be revised and updated termly. It should be part of a wider school crisis management plan and should contain the following:

- Name of key contact who will take charge of dealing with the media (normally the headteacher)
- Location of a room to house the media when they arrive – to avoid an interview/camera team roaming your school building or grounds. (Be aware of health and safety implications when locating the media centre)
- Contact details, including out of hours details, of everyone who might need to be notified – local authority personnel, governors, emergency services. (Crises do not always happen conveniently during school hours)
- A protocol for how students and parents affected will be contacted
- How you plan to keep parents informed before anything appears in the media – they should always be the first to know
- A list of local media contacts

Don't forget to use your school website as a key tool for keeping parents informed. And remember local radio – it's an under-used media tool which offers the opportunity to talk directly to the local community.

When trouble starts

1. Cancel whatever else you are doing.
2. Establish with the media who the school's spokesperson is.
3. Make sure that only the agreed representative speaks to the media.
4. Go public with what you know and stick to the facts. Don't speculate.

Determine the **who, when, what, where, why** and **how** of what has happened.

Communication and **information** are vitally important in these circumstances, so issue regular statements, keep everyone informed and be honest about the situation. There is no point trying to play down the significance of a major fire, for instance, if all the fire engines in town are in the school playground and the roof is about to fall in!

It's worth remembering that if you don't provide the information, then the media are likely to find someone who will.

The 'to do' checklist

- Try to keep the rest of the school informed and running smoothly
- Make sure that everyone gets the same information – students, parents, governors and media representatives – and remember to keep your local education authority, ward councillors and MP in the loop
- Prepare a statement – it should be to the point and factual. Make sure that it includes as much positive information relevant to the incident as possible. For instance refer to any rules or precautions that the school has in place
- Stick to the statement, making clear that this is all the information you have at this point. Be very clear about the information you have and be ready to change the statement if, as is likely, circumstances change. In a crisis circumstances change very fast

Think ahead

Expect media contact out of the blue. Find out what the reporter might know and play for time. Always ring back if you say you will, however difficult it may be. Give yourself time to think through all the issues and consider using the time to rehearse what you are going to say.

- What are the most difficult questions you are likely to be asked?
- How will you answer the questions you hope you don't get?
- What key messages about your school do you want to be sure you get across?

A useful mechanism to consider is drafting a statement but remember to provide the media with regular updates – information flow is very important in a crisis. Bring people on-side by letting them see and understand the decisions that have been made.

It's important that names of those who may have been involved are not released – or confirmed – to anyone before these have been formally agreed and families informed. Refuse requests for photos or school work of children/staff involved.

Taking part in an interview

Make sure you are prepared before you agree to be interviewed. You can reasonably expect to ask certain questions, for instance:

- Who will be doing the interview?
- Will it be just you or will others be there?
- Who will the audience be?
- Is the interview live or pre-recorded?
- What is the first question you will be asked?

Prior to carrying out an interview the interviewer may offer to brief you. Always take up this offer, as they are just doing their job and want to look professional.

Taking part in an interview

Bear in mind the following:

- Keep your answers to the point – don't be evasive and don't get side-tracked
- Say the most important things first, you can always expand if there's time and opportunity
- Avoid jargon and acronyms
- Emphasise the school as a team
- Stay calm and speak slowly and clearly – you can be sympathetic
- If you don't know, say so
- If you are interrupted, politely tell the interviewer you'd like to finish the answer
- Look the interviewer in the eye and don't fidget
- Never blame or complain and always thank people for their support
- If possible, do one-to-one interviews rather than open sessions (press calls) where you're less in control
- If the emergency services are involved, try to do interviews with their representative present – it reinforces the professionalism of the operation

Emergency action list

The following list will help you to prioritise actions in an emergency situation:

	Actions	Responsibility
1	Cancel all other arrangements	
2	Inform the senior management/leadership team and chair of governors	
3	Establish the facts and do not speculate	
4	Immediately contact the nominated media representative and ensure his/her availability	
5	Brief all staff (teaching and non-teaching)	
6	Inform students in classes or groups – remember many students have mobile phones	
7	Inform the director of education, council press office and other key officers	
8	Ensure you are aware of all the facts before speaking to the media	
9	Go public with what you know. If you do not know, it is better to say so than to say nothing or 'no comment'	
10	Inform parents not directly involved using telephone tree and/or letter	
11	If appropriate, provide the media with a designated space on site	
12	Only the nominated media representative should speak to the media	
13	Keep all stakeholders informed	

Emergency action list

	Actions	Responsibility
14	Consider issuing regular statements – brief, factual and correct	
15	The press statement should contain the same key messages that are communicated to staff and parents	
16	Prepare to receive many telephone calls (You might consider putting an answerphone message on your system directing people to the website)	
17	Ensure the school has a clear and efficient system for filtering calls to avoid school telephone lines becoming blocked at a time when you may urgently need to make contact with a range of affected people	
18	Consider publishing regular and up-to-date information on the school website	
19	Set up arrangements to enable accurate information to flow into and out of the school	
20	Set up arrangements to manage visitors	
21	Ensure administrative staff maintain records of all calls received	
22	Maintain regular contact with parents	
23	Evaluate and review the effectiveness of the plan in supporting the media response	

Getting a handle

If you issue 'no comment', reporters will assume you have something to hide and do what they can to get their information from someone else. The last thing you want is rumour spreading as though it were truth, or to be told something you don't know by a journalist.

Stick to saying what you know. Don't speculate and never go off the record. If anything illegal has taken place, the police must be informed. If it's likely that there will be criminal charges, the media is limited in what can be said or written. But don't ever raise this as it antagonises them and you need them on your side!

Support

During a major crisis it's important to get support from others. There are several possibilities:

- Local authority press office
- Professional association
- Other schools
- Unions
- Other relevant professionals

Remember that the media have a job to do and the right to do it. In due course you may want to use them for a variety of reasons. Openness and responsiveness during a crisis can enhance your credibility. You can use this to your school's advantage in the longer term.

Devising and Implementing Your Strategy

 Managing the Media

 Promotional Opportunities

 School Case Studies

 Self-evaluation Tool

Promotional Opportunities

The role of promotional material

Your promotional materials fulfil a vital role, as they are a key way in which people form **judgements** about your school. Self-produced promotional material includes:

- The school prospectus
- School newsletters or magazines
- The school website
- Student and parent handbooks

- Leaflets
- Posters
- Personalised items

Don't underestimate the impression that these documents can create and remember that students can make a major contribution to them. Include students' accounts of trips, workshops, charity fundraising events, athletics successes, etc in your newsletters, use student artwork on your posters and incorporate images of children engaged in a variety of activities on your website.

The school prospectus

The school prospectus is probably your most important promotional tool, so do make sure it does your school justice. There are some key issues to think about:

- The link to other school promotional activities. Your prospectus will be far more effective if its **key messages** are repeated through a range of other school publications, including the website
- Distribution – to whom, when and how?
- What are parents' perceptions of it?
- Are there alternative ways to print that might be either more cost-effective or more forward thinking, such as a CD and DVD versions?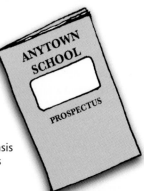
- Do you need to produce some of your information in different languages/formats for the school's different stakeholders?
- The prospectus will need to be updated on a regular basis – this is an important point to consider in costing if it is externally produced

How to produce an effective prospectus

There are some basic principles to follow when creating your prospectus:

- The **quality** of production is as important as the quality of content
- Use a professional photographer and ensure the photographs complement and reflect **key messages**
- Consider the content very carefully – too much text and no-one will read it, so consider publishing a separate parent handbook which provides helpful information to those parents whose children take up a place
- Consider the needs of the parent body – what kind of prospectus would prospective parents want to see? What helps them in their decision-making?
- What about the governing body? Do they want to publish a combined governors' report and school prospectus? Does the prospectus need to serve other governing body requirements?

A number of companies now specialise in producing professional prospectuses and other school materials. We recommend looking at a range of designs that give your school the flexibility of use for other purposes. You may also want to consider inviting a local company to **sponsor** your prospectus.

Regulations and guidance

A school must publish its prospectus at least six weeks before the final date by which parents are asked to apply for admission to the school, or to express a preference for a place. Ensure that copies of the prospectus are made available, if necessary in languages other than English and to people with disabilities. Copies should be available at the school for reference and sent free of charge to parents on request.

Under revised regulations and guidance, school prospectuses have to contain:

- The name, address and telephone number of the school
- The type of school and the names of the headteacher and chair of governors
- Information about admissions
- A statement of the school's ethos and values
- Details of any affiliations with a particular religion or religious denomination; the religious education provided; parents' right to withdraw their child from religious education and collective worship and the alternative provision for those students

Regulations and guidance (cont'd)

- Information about the school's policy on providing for students with special educational needs and any changes to that policy in the last year
- The total number of registered students
- Rates of students' authorised and unauthorised absence
- The school's National Curriculum assessment results at Key Stages 1, 2 (primary schools) and 3 (secondary schools)
- Public examination results – A-levels, vocational qualifications and GCSEs (secondary schools only)
- Student destinations (secondary schools only). A 'Where are they now?' feature can be very effective, creating a more human picture than just statistics

You will want to ensure that prospective parents receive a complete picture of the school and will need to decide whether additional information would be best included in the prospectus or in other school publications.

Design and production

There are a number of key points when planning the **design** of your prospectus:

- Decide what your requirements are from it – eg recruitment of students, information from governors, staff recruitment pack
- Convey clearly the unique selling points/unique perceived benefits of the school through the copy and the photography
- Decide on its main features and structure the prospectus clearly
- Always have the parent/reader in mind when designing layouts
- There should be a simple, eye-catching and tasteful cover
- Ensure that the prospectus has a professional appearance
- Avoid education jargon and ask a governor or member of the support staff to proofread the copy
- Use high quality illustrations/photographs at all times
- Consider the contents of the prospectus carefully. Don't make it too long or include information that dates
- Ensure all contact details are clearly displayed

The school newsletter

Not all schools issue their own regular newsletter, magazine or annual review, yet these are ideal ways of making sure that the stories that you want to print reach a ready and wide audience. And if your school has invested time, effort and money in a high quality prospectus, your other materials need to reflect that same quality.

Your regular newsletter doesn't have to be an expensive, glossy publication but the quality of content does have to match the quality of your prospectus. The best publications look professional; the least effective are pages of bland text dealing with school business and containing spelling and/or grammatical errors.

- Decide on the frequency (weekly, monthly, termly).
- Think about your readers – who is your publication aimed at?
- What are the key messages you want to communicate?
- Is this an information sheet or a **promotional** tool for the school?

If you don't already do so, we recommend publishing an annual review looking back on the school year, using photographs and contributions from students and staff.

Using your school website

Rather like the prospectus and newsletters, your website provides you with a superb platform from which you can promote everything positive about your school. It also provides you with a very easy-to-use mechanism to gain feedback, not only about the website but also about a range of other school matters and/or publications. It needs to be updated regularly with current news and photographs.

In terms of marketing and promoting your school, the electronic design of school information is as important as printed publications. In fact, your website has an advantage over printed material as it has the ability to layer and update content easily and cost effectively. It will provide your school with:

- Access to a wider world – an online school community
- Information that can be constantly and cheaply updated
- A method of communicating directly with existing and prospective stakeholders
- Interactive opportunities
- A research tool

Developing your website

Here are some golden rules for publishing information on the website:

- Update the site regularly
- Use short paragraphs and avoid overcrowded pages
- Include a section highlighting current news and events
- A 'frequently-asked questions' section is a useful mechanism for communicating key messages
- Show the range of extra-curricular and out of school activities, giving broad details of school visits, drama productions, concerts and sports activities
- Invite requests for further information using the email facility
- Use immediate and informal language
- Advertise your website address on **all** school communications
- Publish the school newsletter (or highlights) on the website
- Ensure that any positive press coverage is immediately published
- Use photographs to make the information more interesting. Remember that parental permission will be required if photographs of students are used
- Include a page with links to useful curriculum and related sites, eg DfES

Developing your website

Suggestions for content include:

- Curriculum information
- Newsletters
- School calendar/term dates/examination dates
- Staff recruitment details
- PTA information
- Photographic display
- Gallery of students' work
- School facilities
- Online parental surveys
- A topic/subject/curriculum issue of the week/month
- Student extra-curricular successes eg Duke of Edinburgh scheme, scouts
- Staff news to create a sense of community (marriages, births, successes etc, but all must have staff permission)
- Update on past students – where are they now?

Open events

Open days, open evenings and other school events are excellent opportunities to show off your school to best effect. The way a school presents itself is crucial in terms of **recruiting** prospective students, parents and staff:

- Who's there to meet your visitors, how do they appear and what information do they have available?
- Is the reception area bright and welcoming with a range of appropriate displays?
- Are the grounds and the school building litter free, graffiti free and clean?
- Is it clear to your visitors where to go and who to turn to for information?
- Are there signs to guide them and do the 'meeters and greeters' have badges that identify who they are and the role they are fulfilling at this event?
- Have the key ambassadors for the school – guides, students and all staff (teaching, support and reception) – been well briefed?

Open events

Consider the content of any information pack you may have.
Is it **informative** and **relevant**? Include:

- Your school prospectus
- A map of the school
- Why your school is unique (a few short points)
- A timetable of events
- Some recent newsletters

Make sure you emphasise **positive** messages and, if
the aim of your open event is to recruit students, have
the headteacher describe links with feeder schools and
arrangements for transition.

Use the opportunity to **publicise** any other events that are
taking place and ongoing community links.

Work in your community

Most schools do involve themselves in developing relationships with the local community, especially now that citizenship is becoming so well integrated in schools. Although relationships should not be developed solely for their PR value, do make the most of any opportunities that such activities offer. Consider **developing** and **extending** links with the local community, involving:

- Inviting visitors into school
- Events for the general public
- The use of school premises for local groups
- Inviting people from the community to contribute to curriculum themes
- Church or interfaith links

Work in your community

Examples of newsworthy activities might include:

- Putting on a musical concert in a home for elderly people in the local area
- Becoming involved in a local environmental project
- Holding sporting events in collaboration with other schools and/or local societies
- Working with a community group, eg playgroup, theatre group

Managing the parental grapevine

Many people's impressions about your school are shaped by the strongly-held views of key parents and other community figures. Together, they constitute a powerful 'grapevine' that can work in your favour, but it can also work to counteract the positive messages you're sending out. Like it or not, many parents form opinions about your school based on hearsay and word of mouth.

It's vital to work with these influential-opinion formers but it's not always easy. They may not want to be part of official groups such as the parent-teacher association and sometimes they have a personal agenda which your school cannot support and which can lead to conflict.

It's important to acknowledge the views of these people and try to find some common ground to build on. Engaging with key opinion-formers can be challenging, but endeavour to find ways to work positively together for the good of the school.

Managing the parental grapevine

You can actively manage the grapevine gossip and the people who are generating it. By managing your reputation you can convert parents into positive ambassadors for the school.

- Promote an open door policy. Encourage parents to come to talk to you rather than allow rumours to circulate
- Regularly invite parents into school to take part in focus groups to discuss issues they may have concerns about (ie the issues being talked about in 'outside the gate gossip')
- Take every opportunity to find out what people's concerns are and to put minds at rest. Emphasise the importance of the school's reputation in the local community and the key role influential people can play

Easily missed opportunities

Good opportunities for promoting your school are frequently overlooked.

- Distribute copies of the school newsletter to link schools, libraries, doctors' surgeries, estate agents (even in new show homes) and houses in the local area
- The newsletter can be made available anywhere people gather or sit for any length of time (eg waiting rooms, vets, community centres, cafés, tourist information centres)
- Approach your local supermarket, town hall, community centre or surgery to put up a display about your school using a range of creative well-presented work
- Donate copies of any research work about the local area undertaken by your students to local libraries
- Establish links with key groups in your community – elderly, brownies/guides/scouts, pre-school groups, tertiary/adult colleges, local amateur drama groups, community festival organisers, Chamber of Trade
- Creative use of the school premises out of school hours

Devising and Implementing Your Strategy

 Managing the Media

 Promotional Opportunities

 School Case Studies ◄

 Self-evaluation Tool

School Case Studies

1. Improving a school's media profile

A small, rural comprehensive school in North Yorkshire began a major drive to improve its media profile. Although it did not have a poor image, schools competing with it for student places seemed to be getting more than their fair share of coverage. A press officer was appointed who met with local journalists to see what stories they were interested in and appropriate news releases were then submitted. All staff were encouraged to submit news stories on a standard form; this generated many leads. Slowly, coverage of the school began to increase in the local and regional press.

A few years later the school hit the PR jackpot with a story about a boy who in 12 years had never missed a day at school. This resulted in full-page stories in most national tabloids, a slot on Radio 5 Live and even a story on Sky News. The positive media attention given to the school that week would have cost tens of thousands of pounds, and resulted in huge interest from parents and students alike. A school magazine, edited by the press officer and written mainly by students, was established to generate community interest and allow the school to promote good news on a regular basis.

2. Gaining a national reputation for innovative work

A secondary school in a former mining community in South Yorkshire managed to gain a national reputation for its innovative work by utilising a variety of avenues to get itself on the public stage.

The school won a number of awards and competitions for environmental projects. This created considerable media interest, which spurred the school on to even more high profile projects, such as building its own wind turbine to power a micro river system. A major feature in the Times Educational Supplement resulted in the key member of staff being invited to speak at a number of national conferences about the school's work.

The latest venture involved students in year 10 visiting Lesotho in Southern Africa as part of a £30,000 project to build a wind turbine for a small village. It will bring power to that village for the first time. This project earned the school its own slot on the local BBC news programme and the project organiser a major award for his efforts. The school now enjoys an enviable reputation for its high quality citizenship work.

3. Managing community perceptions of a merger

A separate infant and junior school in Outer London was able to re-launch itself very successfully as an all-through primary school with attached nursery, thanks to a strategic approach to managing community perceptions.

A strategy was devised to promote the newly-merged school and to raise its profile within a community unhappy with the amalgamation. A range of promotional material was produced, including a new prospectus, parent handbook and a leaflet for wide distribution. A press schedule was compiled for the academic year and a new website created to forge closer partnerships with the local community and businesses. A new building was built to link the two previously separate sites, local companies came forward to sponsor the football team kit and family fun days were organised.

4. Changing perceptions and increasing roll

This secondary school in Greater London experienced a major transformation, gaining increasing popularity within its community. Student applications increased dramatically with significant numbers actively selecting it as their school of choice.

The school had excellent staff, very good practice, great facilities and a strong ethos. However, its reputation locally was poor. Students came from across a wide area, many joining the school because there were no spaces elsewhere. The challenge was to sustain a long-term marketing strategy that would counteract local perceptions and increase the number of local students selecting the school as a first choice.

The school embraced a short, medium and long-term strategy that ensured it had a plan of activities and events supported by a press campaign. Primary school students were invited into school to take part in exciting curriculum-based activities that they would not experience in their own school. These regular visits began to build up a long-term identification with, and loyalty to, the school. As the positive good news stories/press coverage built up, staff and students began to truly believe in themselves as part of an excellent school.

5. Improving internal communications

This South West London secondary school was in special measures and undergoing regular HMI monitoring visits. Staff, under enormous pressure to perform at all levels, felt demoralised and exhausted. The school was successful in transforming the prevailing culture. Student attitude and behaviour improved, staff morale increased and the school ethos became far more positive.

The marketing strategy aimed to:

- Promote the new headteacher to the local community and primary schools prior to the start of the new academic year
- Ensure that all school publications were in place for the new academic year
- Engage the staff in the process and ensure that they felt valued and a part of the changes that needed to be made at the school

To ensure that open communications were initiated with all key internal stakeholders, focus groups were run for staff, students and parents. The headteacher ensured that staff felt valued by celebrating each stage of successful progress, including providing regular wellbeing sessions.

5. Improving internal communications

6. Parent power

This church school in Greater London – one that took students from a wide catchment area and was experiencing serious problems with discipline and poor results – succeeded in becoming a significantly over-subscribed local school.

Locally, the school had been shunned by parents and was held in poor regard by the community. As a result of a dramatically falling roll, it faced closure. In order to ensure its own survival, the school initiated a marketing strategy that focused on building a relationship with local prospective parents, so that they became part of shaping the future of the school for their children.

Prospective families (parents, younger siblings, grandparents) were invited into school for special family days. The school demonstrated its commitment to working with parents by encouraging prospective parents to join working groups and become part of the decision-making process and the future of the school. Parental involvement included task groups deciding on a new school uniform, homework policy, community links, home/school links and extra-curricular activities.

7. Promoting the school

This small primary school in Greater London had been experiencing a steady fall in numbers and poor SATs results with recent changes to the senior management team and a loss of parental confidence. It used every opportunity in the autumn term to attract students for the following academic year and succeeded in winning the confidence of existing and prospective parents. It is now oversubscribed.

The school's unique selling point was its small numbers, enabling it to work more individually with parents and students. A parents' handbook was produced and every child was provided with their own individual learning file. This included certificates, school reports and an individual learning plan. Parents were delighted with the new document as it provided them with a portfolio and personal record of their child's primary school life. A date was agreed for the school open morning for prospective parents and, as the school was located on a busy road, an 18ft banner was displayed on the school fence, advertising the date and time. The school used the open morning to promote its new approach to monitoring the students' learning.

8. Community newsletter

A secondary school in Stockport now achieves great marketing value from its community newsletter which is issued twice a term and delivered inside a local free newspaper to over 12,000 homes. The A4 double-sided newsletter was introduced ten years ago and covers community issues as well as curricular, social and sporting information about the school. It is remarkably easy to compile, with the school's marketing and publicity officer coordinating the effort. This includes liaison with six feeder primary schools via email, and, within the school, using a proforma to key staff with the instruction that contributions be limited to 100 words.

The headteacher's editorial forms the basis of the newsletter, which usually carries about 30 news items including information on local charities and former students. School fundraising activities are always publicised and as many names of individual students as possible are included to ensure the copy appeals to parents and students. The cost, using the school's printing machine, is £150 per issue. On publication day copies are given to students, as well as being sent to local libraries, the Civic Hall and to feeder primary schools.

Devising and Implementing Your Strategy

 Managing the Media

 Promotional Opportunities

 School Case Studies

 Self-evaluation Tool

Self-evaluation Tool

Self-evaluation Tool

The aim of this self-evaluation tool is to help you:

- Judge the current level you have reached with your marketing/PR work, thereby providing a baseline for future comparison
- Identify which areas of your work need improvement
- Identify the actions that you need to move forward
- Judge progress in six months' or a year's time

The tables on the following pages are self-explanatory, with a tick needed in the appropriate box as follows:

0 = you feel you have not begun to address the question
1 = you have started work, but it is in its early stages
2 = you feel quite confident about the work you've done in this area
3 = you feel the work you have done in this area represents excellent practice

We have included numerical values for each response so that, if you wish to, you can use statistics and charts to assess your performance quite analytically.

Getting started

Getting started	◁ Emerging		Advanced ▷	
	0	**1**	**2**	**3**
Are you clear about the marketing and communications issues facing the school?				
Have you identified your target audience?				
Are senior management and governors fully behind the work?				

Getting started score: ☐ /9 = ☐ %

Vision

Vision	◁ Emerging		Advanced ▷	
	0	1	2	3
Do you have an agreed vision for your school?				
Has the vision benefited from the input of diverse stakeholders?				
Have you shared the vision with key stakeholders?				
Have you used your vision to set aims and objectives?				

Vision score: [/12] = [%]

Devising your marketing/PR strategy

Devising your marketing/PR strategy	◁ Emerging 0	1	Advanced ▷ 2	3
Are you aware of the marketing work done at the school to date?				
Do you feel this has been shared with all staff?				
Have comments been requested from all staff?				
Have you devised a comprehensive marketing strategy?				
Is your strategy linked in with the school improvement/development plan?				

Devising your marketing/PR strategy score: ☐ /15 = ☐ %

Unique features and mission statement

Unique features and mission statement	◁ Emerging		Advanced ▷	
	0	1	2	3
Have you carried out a SWOT analysis to identify the unique features of your school?				
Do you ensure that the unique features of your school are reflected in all publicity materials?				
Have you devised a mission statement?				
Have you communicated your mission statement to all key stakeholders?				
Do staff recognise their role in advocating your school's unique features and mission statement?				

Unique features and mission statement score: ☐ /15 = ☐ %

Auditing

Auditing	Emerging 0	1	Advanced 2	3
Have you considered your existing marketing work?				
Have you audited your existing public profile?				
Have you used a variety of sources of evidence to form audit judgements?				
Does your auditing include staff and student morale?				
Does the school ensure that all events are evaluated, eg critical friend analysis of open events?				

Auditing score: ☐ /15 = ☐ %

Staffing

Staffing	◁ Emerging Advanced ▷			
	0	1	2	3
Do you have a nominated person in place to oversee marketing/PR?				
Is there a team in place to work with the nominated person?				
Do the school staff know what their roles are with respect to marketing/PR?				
Has the marketing/PR group benefited from training?				

Staffing score: ☐ /12 = ☐ %

Aims, objectives and action planning

Aims, objectives and action planning	◁ Emerging		Advanced ▷	
	0	1	2	3
Have you identified and written down clear aims and objectives for your marketing work?				
Have you identified specific actions to meet the stated objectives?				
Does your school have an up-to-date calendar?				
Have you considered when publications should be produced and distributed, based around key statutory dates/open events?				
Does your school have a structure for communicating good news stories, internally and externally?				
Does your school plan events, publications, press releases at least a term in advance?				

Aims, objectives and action planning score: ☐/18 = ☐%

Working with parents

Working with parents	Emerging 0	1	Advanced 2	3
Do you regularly consult and act upon parents' views?				
Do you have strategies in place for consulting 'hard to reach' groups?				
Do you feel that the school meets the expectation of parents?				
How well do you feel the school's partnership with parents supports learning at home and at school?				
Does the school have shared procedures for dealing with parents' concerns and complaints?				
How do you gather the views of other stakeholders?				
How do you share feedback with parents and other stakeholders?				

Working with parents score: [/21] = [%]

Media work

Media work	<Emerging		Advanced>	
	0	1	2	3
To what extent do you have a comprehensive, up-to-date media contacts list?				
Do you have one named press/media contact at your school?				
Do you issue regular press releases?				
Do you monitor your school's press coverage in an analytical way?				
Have you exploited radio and television to promote your school?				
Do you hold regular press events to try to get media coverage?				
Do you have a media crisis plan that is regularly reviewed?				

Media work score: /21 =   %

School prospectus and associated publications

School prospectus and associated publications	Emerging 0	1	Advanced 2	3
Does the school have an up to date prospectus?				
Does it comply with statutory regulations?				
Does it fully inform parents about the school's vision and ethos?				
Is there an indexed photographic library of quality school photographs?				
Do you have photography permission forms from all your students/staff and a list of children who should not appear in photographs?				
Have you explored all the school (and governors') requirements for publications to ensure cost-effective printing of prospectus etc.				
Does the school have copies of a range of materials from neighbouring schools?				

School prospectus and associated publications score: ⬚ /21 = ⬚ %

Communication network

Communication network	Emerging		Advanced	
	0	1	2	3
Have you set up an effective communications network in your school?				
Have you identified the school's range of target audiences?				
Do you have a circulation list for all the school's publications?				
Have you identified any gaps in the range of audiences that you would like to reach?				
Does the school receptionist /admissions officer ask how enquirers have found out about your school?				
Is there a system in place to monitor feedback from the target audiences that see your school's information (website, publications, etc)?				
Have you clarified the methods of communication with this group?				

Communication network score: ☐ /21 = ☐ %

Other promotional opportunities

Other promotional opportunities	Emerging 0	1	Advanced 2	3
Do you have a regular school newsletter, magazine or review?				
Do you use your school website to promote your school?				
Do you use open days and evenings to promote your school?				
Do you consider marketing during student visits to your school?				
Do you use advertising to publicise your school's open events?				
Do you reach out to the community to promote your school?				

Other promotional opportunities score: [/18] = [%]

Monitoring and evaluation

Monitoring and evaluation	◁ Emerging		Advanced ▷	
	0	1	2	3
Do you monitor your marketing/PR work to keep track of progress?				
Do you evaluate your marketing/PR work to judge effectiveness?				
Do you use evaluation to modify actions in future?				

Monitoring and evaluation score: ☐ /9 = ☐ %

KEY
0-29%   emerging school
30-59%   established school
60-89%   advanced school
90%+   cutting edge school

TOTAL SCORE: ☐ /207 = ☐ %

Date evaluation was carried out: ☐ / ☐ / ☐

Websites and books

Institute of Marketing: **www.cim.co.uk**
Institute of Fundraising: **www.institute-of-fundraising.org.uk**
GDA training manual: **www.grebotdonnelly.com**
Croner: **www.croner.co.uk**
Heist: **www.heist.co.uk**
Educational Communications (sponsorship): **www.edcoms.com**

Pathways to Child Friendly Schools – A Guide for Parents by Fiona Carnie
Published by Human Scale Education, (2004)

A marketing association

keys2marketing is a marketing association for maintained schools in the UK.
It provides advice, support and training on all aspects of marketing and
communications, including reputation management, organisational
development/improvement and sponsorship/grant opportunities.

Membership gives access to resources and expertise in public relations and to a forum
in which to gain knowledge, share experience and benefit from networking
opportunities.

k2m is endorsed and supported by the London Challenge Team and the DfES.
For further information visit: www.keys2marketing.org.uk

Acknowledgements

Brin Best
I am grateful to Trevor Wear at Settle High School & Community College, who gave me the opportunity to learn the ropes of school marketing and PR during my time on his staff.

Isabella Donnelly and Macia Grebot
We would like to thank colleagues with whom we have pioneered some of our work and who understand the impact that effective marketing and communications has on all aspects of organisational improvement and development.

Gill O'Donnell made numerous helpful comments on an earlier draft of the book, based on her experience as development officer in a vibrant secondary school. Linda Edge provided valuable editorial support and made numerous helpful suggestions that improved the content of the book.

We are grateful to the schools who are featured in the case studies, whose work demonstrates what is possible when promoting your school.

About the authors

Brin Best BSc (hons), PGCE, FRGS, FMA, MCIJ is managing director of Innovation for Education Ltd, an education training and consultancy company based in Yorkshire. Prior to setting up the company, he worked as a teacher and manager in schools and local education authorities for ten years, and was the marketing and PR officer of a thriving secondary school in North Yorkshire. Brin is a member of the Chartered Institute of Journalists and is series consultant for Teachers' Pocketbooks.

He may be contacted at:
Innovation for Education Ltd, 6 Manor Square, Otley, LS21 3AP
Tel. +44 (0) 1943 466994   Fax +44 (0) 1943 465550
Email: office@innovation4education.co.uk
Website: www.innovation4education.co.uk

About the authors

Isabella Donnelly DipM MCIM is a director of Grebot Donnelly Associates, a marketing consultancy specialising in the education sector. Isabella has diplomas in both marketing and business studies and has worked in the marketing field for over 20 years, both in the commercial and education sector. She has worked at both LEA and school level devising and implementing successful marketing and communications strategies.

Macia Grebot BEd (hons), NPQH is a director of Grebot Donnelly Associates. She has a school-based background, with extensive experience at senior management level in the maintained and special sector as well as in LEA school improvement. She is the author of a series of articles on marketing for schools for the education press. Macia is a performance management consultant and European Foundation for Quality Management assessor.

Marcia and Isabella may be contacted at:
Grebot Donnelly Associates,
GDA House, 1 The Mews, Bridge Road, St Margarets, Twickenham TW1 1RE
Tel. +44 020 8332 0400   Fax + 44 020 8332 1177
Email: info@grebotdonnelly.com   Website: www.grebotdonnelly.com

Order Form

Your details

Name _____

Position _____

School _____

Address _____

_____

_____

Telephone _____

Fax _____

E-mail _____

VAT No. (EC only) _____

Your Order Ref _____

Please send me:

		No. copies
Promoting Your School	Pocketbook	☐
_____	Pocketbook	☐
_____	Pocketbook	☐
_____	Pocketbook	☐
_____	Pocketbook	☐

Order by Post

Teachers' Pocketbooks

Laurel House, Station Approach
Alresford, Hants. SO24 9JH UK

Order by Phone, Fax or Internet

Telephone: +44 (0)1962 735573
Facsimile: +44 (0)1962 733637
E-mail: sales@teacherspocketbooks.co.uk
Web: www.teacherspocketbooks.co.uk

Pocketbooks

Teachers' Titles:

- A-Z of Educational Terms
- Accelerated Learning
- Behaviour Management
- Creative Teaching
- Dyslexia
- Form Tutor's
- Fundraising for Schools
- Head of Department's
- ICT in the Classroom
- Inclusion
- Learning to Learn
- Managing Workload
- Mentoring in Schools
- Primary Headteacher's
- Primary Teacher's
- Promoting Your School
- Secondary Teacher's
- Stop Bullying
- Teaching Assistant's
- Trips & Visits

Selected Management Titles:

- Appraisals
- Assertiveness
- Career Transition
- Challenger's
- Coaching
- Communicator's
- Controlling Absenteeism
- Decision-making
- Developing People
- Discipline
- Emotional Intelligence
- Empowerment
- Energy & Well-being
- Icebreakers
- Impact & Presence
- Influencing
- Interviewer's
- Leadership
- Learner's
- Managing Budgets
- Managing Change
- Managing Your Appraisal
- Meetings
- Mentoring
- Motivation
- Negotiator's
- NLP
- Openers & Closers
- People Manager's
- Performance Management
- Personal Success
- Positive Mental Attitude
- Presentations
- Problem Behaviour
- Project Management
- Resolving Conflict
- Succeeding at Interviews
- Self-managed Developmen
- Stress
- Teamworking
- Thinker's
- Time Management
- Trainer's
- Vocal Skills